The Small World Recipe Book
50 Exciting Ideas For Small World Play

ACKNOWLEDGEMENTS

Written by: Helen Bromley

Illustrated by: Peter Scott

Produced by: Lynda Lawrence.

Published by: Lawrence Educational Publications
                       Unit 21, Brookvale Trading Estate, Moor Lane,
                       Birmingham, West Midlands B6 7AQ.

                       © Lawrence Educational 2004

ISBN: 978-1-903670-39-2

Introduction

Small world play provides a stimulating and meaningful context in which all areas of the Early Years Curriculum can be developed. It excites, emboldens and empowers. Children can share knowledge that they already possess whilst at the same time being involved in the creation of new knowledge and understandings alongside their friends and companions. Through being invited into another world, young learners can be inspired and their imaginations developed. This kind of activity gives children time to experiment, create and reflect.

For many children, small world play will be a very significant experience indeed, offering them control over the miniature environment, and the opportunity to become deeply engaged in an activity for long periods of time. Playing with and exploring the small worlds involves the children in investigating both objects and materials through the use of their senses, finding out about and identifying features of living things, objects and events that they observe. If you involve the children in creating their own worlds, they will be able to construct an environment over which they have complete ownership, and will have to make choices and decisions about the appropriateness of the available resources.

This book is intended to inspire practitioners to create a range of innovative and unusual small worlds using a wide variety of materials. Within the recipes you will hopefully find some ideas that are new to you as well as some slightly different slants on old favourites. Don't worry if the children reorganise your initial arrangement when they come to use the small world – that is what small world play is all about! The more you involve the children in setting up the small worlds, the less you will be concerned about such issues!

Above all else, please remember that the main ingredient of all these recipes should be the imaginations of the children that you work with. Let them use it liberally!

Helen Bromley

How to use this book

On the following three pages you will find suggestions for the three main components of small world – the containers, the surfaces and the inhabitants! These lists are not intended to be exhaustive, but instead offer a wide range of possibilities for starting points. They are also designed to act as reminders and memory joggers to transport you to small worlds that you may have created once, but had forgotten about. I hope that you will also meet some new ideas; suggestions for unusual or little used resources which would bring a whole new dimension to the children's play.

Altogether, the lists provide you with a staggering 125,000 combinations of bases, surfaces and inhabitants – so you need never be short of a new idea for small world play!

You might like to use the lists for an audit of the resources currently available for small world play in your setting. Do you have a variety of containers? Are the surfaces provided for the children sufficiently diverse to help enrich their vocabulary and promote creative thinking? Do you offer the children the opportunity to work with a variety of toy animals, both real and imagined? Are the resources accessible so that the children can create their own small worlds? Do you have any animals in large numbers – a herd of elephants, for example, offers many more play opportunities than just one or two. How can you transform the children's perception of the most popular small world figures? Are the dinosaurs always in wet sand – or can you devise other environments that will create more imaginative possibilities?

Following the lists of resources you will find 50 recipes for small worlds, and descriptions of how they might be created. Like any good recipe, they are intended to be flexible enough for you to change the quantities required, and indeed, the ingredients and utensils themselves! Please don't feel that you have to wait until you have all the ingredients before setting out to create the environment suggested; substitutions and additions of your own will create even more possibilities. It is also worth remembering that the vast majority of ideas listed in this book can be used outdoors as well as inside. The weather of the day will add a whole new set of potential learning opportunities.

Where appropriate, you will find a 'recommended read' at the foot of the page. The book suggested links to the small world on that page and if read to the children will enhance their story language and offer a model for their own stories. However, it is important to remember that the children's own ideas hold paramount importance here! Retelling stories through small world play is undoubtedly valuable, and gives children the opportunity to become deeply engaged with the language of narrative and of story structure, but it is important to remember that this is just one small aspect of small world play.

You may wish to treat this book as a working document, adding your own ideas and observations to particular pages that have inspired you. Don't forget to take photographs of small worlds that are particularly successful, so that you have a record of your and the children's achievements.   Above all else – enjoy yourself!

Small World containers and bases

Builder's Tray	Flowerpot Saucer	Teapot	Fabric Remnant	Lidded snack pot
Gravel Tray	Rug	Large Shell	Thermal Blanket	Cane Wigwam
Growbag Tray	Carpet Tile	Shoebox	Tea Tray	Flowerpot
Potting on Tray	Carpet Sample	Jelly Mould	Hat	Pipes, hoses, tubes
Washing up bowl	Mirror Tile	Cushion Cover	Hollowed out book	Shoe or boot
Wickerwork shell	Under–the– bed–box	Baking tray	Piece of hardboard	Aquarium
Matchbox	Detergent Tablet box	Film pot	Supermarket fruit tray	Ceramic tile
Goldfish bowl	Basket	Cardboard egg tray	Handbag	Doormat
Biscuit tin	Wicker ball	Coconut Shell	Hoop	Wooden barrel
Garden trug	Wooden casket	Suitcase	Box with drawers	Chocolate box

Small world surfaces

Dry Sand	Pea shingle	Greengrocer's grass	Crazy soap	Cold water
Wet sand	Coloured gravel	Hessian	Mud	Warm water
Coloured sand	Coir	Bubble wrap	Compost	Coloured water
Sand mixed with glitter	Pebbles	Shaving foam	Bark chippings	Water and glitter
Ice cubes	Ice blocks	Pebbles	Composted bark	Moss
Silver foil	Shaving foam	Soap flakes(dry)	Soap flakes and water	Hay
Straw	Cous cous	Jelly	Cornflour mixture	Dog biscuits
Seeds	Dried peas	Feathers	Shells	Wood shavings
Shredded paper	Pulses	Pasta	Grain	Tinsel
Polystyrene chips	Glass nuggets	Wadding	Cotton wool	Modroc

Small World Inhabitants

Dinosaurs	Storybook characters	Ants	Worms	Trucks
Cars	Butterflies	Bees	Spiders	Mice
Aeroplanes	Cars	Diggers	Tractors	Trains
Elephants	Pigs	Unicorns	Dragons	Snakes
Tortoises	Fish	Sharks	Octopi	Knights
Royalty	Ducks	Frogs	Clockwork toys	Mermaids
Pets	Bears	Lizards	Ladybirds	Cows
Seahorses	Horses	Penguins	Polar Bears	Whales
Boats	Submarines	Bicycles	Witches	Wizards
Fairies	Children	Birds	Rabbits	Astronauts

RECIPE 1

The Garden Pond

Ingredients:
- Flowerpot Saucer
- Artificial water lilies and pondweed
- Toy frogs, fish, etc
- Small amount of gravel or pea shingle
- Water
- Small amount of bubble wrap (optional)

Method:
Place the gravel or pea shingle on the bottom of the flowerpot saucer.
Pour the water in gently. Add the artificial water lilies and pondweed. Finally add the fish and the frogs to their new home. Should you wish to make it look as if there is frogspawn in the pond, cut some bubble wrap into an appropriate shape. Add some black dots with a spirit based, water proof marker pen, and place it in the water.

Why not…
Use food colouring to tint the water blue or green.
Position a toy cat so that it looks like it is watching the contents of the pond with great concentration! Watch for the reaction of the children.

Recommended Read: Growing Frogs, by Meredith Hooper, Walker Books, ISBN 0744578191

RECIPE 2

Teddy Bear's Picnic

Ingredients:
- Builder's Tray
- Greengrocer's grass or similar green fabric
- Some Teddy Bears – a mixture of sizes would be good.
- Doll's Tea Set
- A piece of material to represent a picnic rug, large enough for the bears to sit on.
- Some small pots of bedding plants, if desired

Method:
Spread the greengrocer's grass out so that it completely covers the black surface of the builder's tray. Position the pots of bedding plants, if being used, around the edge of the tray. Add the bears, the rug and the tea set.

Why not...
Make some picnic food for the bears using salt dough.
Plan a real teddy bear's picnic with the children. Don't forget to invite their bears along too.

Recommended Read: The Walker Book of Bear Stories, Walker Books, ISBN 0744588758

RECIPE 3

The Hard Shell

Ingredients:
- 1 reasonably large shell – a conch or similar
- A flowerpot saucer
- Dry sand
- Small figures/creatures e.g. seahorses, mermaids, sea dragons….

Method:
Spread the sand across the bottom of the flowerpot saucer and wedge the shell into it so that the large opening in the shell resembles a cave. Add the toy figures.

Why not…
Pop just one toy crab into the shell; encourage the children to tell the story of how he got to be living in such a place, or stories of the things that he has seen.
Add some jewels at the back of the shell, and some pirates at the front to guard them!
If you have more than one shell available then you could have different characters living in each of them, increasing the storying opportunities.

Recommended Read: Old Shell, New Shell by Helen Ward, Templar, ISBN 1840119039

Skating rink

Ingredients:
- Shallow tray or flowerpot saucer
- Water
- Play people
- Silver foil

Method:
First, line the shallow tray or the flowerpot saucer with foil.
Then part fill it with water and place in the freezer overnight.
Show the children how to skate the play people across the rink.
Obviously this small world is a temporary one!

Why not…
Add glitter or food colouring to the water before freezing.
Discuss the changes that take place as the skating rink melts.

RECIPE 5

Volcanic Island

Ingredients:
- Piece of hardboard
- Chicken wire
- Lots of old newspapers
- Wallpaper paste
- Paint
- PVA Glue

Method:
Fashion the chicken wire into the shape of a volcano, and place it onto the hardboard. Ensure that you create a crater at the heart of the volcano, so that flames can erupt from it! Make up the wallpaper paste, and using the newspaper, begin to build up layers of papier-mâché onto the chicken wire volcano. Involve the children in this activity, as they are sure to enjoy it. When you feel that you have enough layers, allow the papier- mache to dry.
Next, paint the volcano in suitable colours. You may wish to paint the inside of the volcano in hot shades, perhaps adding tissue paper flames pouring from the top.
When the paint is dry, varnish the volcano with PVA glue mixed with water. When the glue is dry, your volcano is ready for use.

Why not….
Use dinosaurs with your volcano, adding some real rocks or pebbles in the foothills for added impact.
Place brightly coloured sand, mixed with glitter at the base of the volcano.
Use the papier-mâché and chicken wire method to create other structures such as mountains, hills or caves.

RECIPE 6

In the field

Ingredients:
- A green rug
- Some cuddly toy rabbits. Mixed sizes would be good, but is not absolutely necessary
- Some artificial flowers
- Leaf skeletons

Method:
Spread out the rug and add the rabbits, the artificial flowers and the leaf skeletons.

Why not…
Offer the children some flowerpots or pieces of drainpipe to place under the rug, so that the rabbits can have a burrow.

RECIPE 7

Surprise, surprise

Ingredients:
- Small, empty, cylindrical plastic lidded pots that usually contain potato snacks.
- Small pieces of fabric or tissue. (Net, gauze, or similarly fine fabrics would be ideal)
- Collection of tiny figures or creatures.

Method:
Cover the outside of the pot with attractive paper or fabric; so that it's original purpose is disguised.
Place the fabric and a selection of tiny figures in the pot.

Why not…
Put together a collection of such pots so that children can choose their favourites.
Perhaps you could lend them out for parents and children to use together at home.
Adding buttons, sequins and ribbons would give added possibilities to the play.

RECIPE 8

Down on the farm

Ingredients:
- Selection of rugs and carpet tiles of different colours and textures, including stiff bristle rugs to represent ploughed fields.
- Tractors, combine harvesters etc
- Farm animals
- Play people

Method:
Spread the rugs and carpet tiles out to represent the farmer's fields. Add the vehicles, animals, and people.

Why not….
Add some scarves or strips of fabric to form rivers, lakes or streams.
Combine with block play, so that the children are encouraged to design the farm buildings.

Recommended Read: Farmer Duck, by Martin Waddell, Walker Books, ISBN 0744581737

RECIPE 9

Tell us a story

Ingredients:
- A cushion cover with a picture or series of pictures on it.
- A selection of toys that reflect the pictures on the cushion cover.

Method:
Talk through the pictures on the cushion cover with the children and, with their help, make up a story based around the images shown. Involve the children by getting them to act out the story with the props provided.
Make the cushion cover and props available for the children's use, so that they can invent stories of their own.

Why not…
Keep the toys and/or objects inside the cushion cover, so that you have an instant storytelling resource.
Have a selection of cushion covers and accompanying resources available
Begin to use cushion covers with a more abstract design as a context for small world play.

RECIPE 10

Planetary Patrol

Ingredients:

- One shiny Thermal Blanket, the sort available from camping shops.
- Some astronaut puppets, and toy space monsters if possible.
- Spheres of all kinds, to represent planets.
- Large sequin stars or similar

Method:

Spread the Thermal Blanket out, either on the floor or on a tabletop.
Add the puppets and spheres. Sprinkle liberally with the stars.

Why not…

Add some simple percussion instruments so that the children can make space music.
Encourage the children to make some flying saucers from paper plates to add to the environment

Recommended Read; Martian Rock by Carol Diggory Shields, Walker Books, ISBN 0744578590

RECIPE 11

Just Deserts

Ingredients:

- Grow bag tray
- Coloured gravel
- Dry sand
- A mirror tile
- Some toy camels, or other desert dwelling animals and people

Method:

Sprinkle the sand throughout the growbag tray, and add the coloured gravel where you feel it would be appropriate.

Make a space in the sand/gravel mix and place the mirror tile in it.

Add the camels, or other chosen desert inhabitants.

Why not…

Add pipe cleaner palm trees made by the children to create an oasis. Add a magic carpet, for an air of mystery.

RECIPE 12

Snow business

Ingredients:

- Shallow Plastic Tea Tray
- Crazy Soap
- Play people
- Small fir trees, sledges etc., from a cake decorating shop

Method:

Squirt the crazy soap onto the tray. Build up a reasonable amount.

Crazy soap can easily be moulded, so the children might like to make it into hills or snowballs; a snow cave would even be possible! Now add the figures, trees and any other suitable objects. Sprinkle with glitter for a touch of magic.

Why not…

Leave this small world out where parents can see it, as it is the type of activity that could easily be replicated at home.

Add some little children's novelty nailbrushes shaped either like whales or boats, for added interest

Recommended Read: Snow, by Manya Stojic, David Bennett, ISBN 1856024423

RECIPE 13

Beach Life

Ingredients:
- Builder's tray
- Sand
- Shells, pebbles
- Play people
- Water
- Small pots and spoons
- Paper and matchsticks for making flags

Method:
Place the sand over one half of the tray. Pour water in the other half, so that you have a representation of both the beach and the sea. Add the shells and play people. Keep the tiny pots and spoons nearby so that children can make sand castles in miniature. You can also suggest that they make a flag for their sandcastle from matchsticks and tiny pieces of paper.

Why not…
Keep some beach books nearby. Maps and guides from seaside towns would be good.
Have some blank postcards available so that the children can send them on behalf of the characters in the small world.

Recommended Read: Come Away From the Water Shirley, by John Burningham, Red Fox, 09989940X

RECIPE 14

Bear Necessities

Ingredients:
- Potting up tray
- Twigs, branches
- Autumn leaves, when available
- Toy bears, preferably in a variety of sizes.
- Small rocks
- Composted bark
- Two or three miniature conifers, if desired

Method:
Spread the composted bark over the surface of the tray.
Add the leaves, twigs, branches and rocks. If using, add the miniature conifers and arrange them in the environment.
Finally, add the bears.

Why not…
Replace the composted bark with cotton wool, to create a snowy scene. Provide enough rocks and pebbles, or block play equipment so that the children can build the bears a cave for the hibernation season.

Recommended Read: Let's Go Home Little Bear, by Martin Waddell, Walker Books, ISBN 0744572975

RECIPE 15

Butterflies and bees

Ingredients:
A cane 'wigwam' – the sort used to support climbing plants
Materials for weaving – raffia, string, vines, crepe paper etc
Artificial flowers
Toy butterflies and bees

Method:
Weave the chosen material around the cane wigwam with the children, creating a variety of patterns and textures with the different bits and pieces. When you have finished weaving, add the artificial flowers, the butterflies and the bees.

Why not…
Use this small world outdoors as well as inside.
Thread small mirrors on strong nylon thread and add them to the woven structure.

Recommended Read: Caterpillar, Butterfly, Vivian French, Walker Books, ISBN 0744562821

RECIPE 16

If you go down to the woods today

Ingredients:

- Builder's tray
- Composted bark
- Selection of miniature conifers
- Wood dwelling toy animals e.g. foxes, badgers, squirrels, deer, etc
- Pieces of bark, twigs
- Acorns, conkers, beechnuts, pine cones – according to season and availability!

Method:
Spread the composted bark throughout the builder's tray. Position the conifers. Add the pieces of bark and the twigs. Sprinkle with acorns, pine cones, etc Add the animals.

Why not…
Add 1 fox, 2 squirrels, 3 badgers, 4 acorns, etc and make a woodland counting book, by taking photographs of the objects

Recommended Read: The Happy Hedgehog Band, Martin Waddell, Walker Books, ISBN 0744530490

RECIPE 17

Pipe Dreams

Ingredients:
- A selection of tubes, flexible and inflexible. The collection might include pieces of piping with different diameters, lengths of flexible hose.
- Dry sand and damp sand
- Snakes, bugs, other tiny creatures that could fit through the tubes.
- Builder's Tray or similar

Method:

Spread some dry sand over the bottom of the Builder's Tray. Then layer tubes, pipes and hoses with the damp sand, until you are happy with the structure that you have created. Add the creatures. You may wish to hide some of them so that the children can discover them for themselves.

Why not…

Get the children to help you build the structure. It would be a wonderful context for using the language of mathematics to solve problems.

Make sure that you allow the children to remake the structure to suit the needs of their play.

RECIPE 18

A Hole In the Ground

Ingredients:

- Spare patch of ground outside the setting
- Child friendly spades, trowels, etc.
- Piece of pond lining material
- Water
- Selection of plastic animals, people and vehicles.

Method:

Working with the children, create a hole in the ground of a suitable size for some small world play. Use the spare earth from the hole to create hills, mountains; whatever the children feel is appropriate. Show them how to line the hole with the pond liner and add water. You might wish to secure the liner into its position with smooth pebbles or logs.

The next step is to bring the small world to life by adding its inhabitants. Have a good selection available so that the children can choose what kind of transformation that bring about. So many possibilities exist – from dinosaurs, to lakes with boats, from African water holes to swimming pools…

Why not…

Photograph the results of the children's experimentation, and display them in a photo album with their comments, for parents and carers to see.

Recommended Read: The Dog that Dug, Jonathan Long and Korky Paul, Red Fox ISBN 0099986108

Glow in the Dark

Ingredients:
- A large piece of thick black fabric
- A small table
- A collection of glow in the dark animals, skeletons, etc
- Some glow in the dark stars, moons, planets etc
- A torch – or two!

Method:
Drape the dark fabric over the small table, leaving a fold at the front, which would give access to the children.
Add the creatures, skeletons, moons and stars and torches!

Why not…
Make your own collection of fluorescent creatures and other objects, by purchasing some glow in the dark paint!

Recommended Read: Funnybones by Janet and Allan Ahlberg, Puffin Books, ISBN 0140565817

RECIPE 20

Teeny tiny

Ingredients:
- A matchbox
- Tiny pieces of fabric that can fold up easily – e.g net, gauze, etc
- Some very small toys
- A very tiny shell or pebble (optional)
- Sequins or glitter (optional)

Method:
Make up a tiny small world in a matchbox for the children to see. You might ask them to guess what is inside the matchbox before revealing its contents. The children are sure to be intrigued by this, so it might be a good idea to have more than one available after the activity has been introduced!

Why not…
- Make some matchbox small worlds from objects found outdoors
- If you can collect enough matchboxes, consider the possibility of the children making a matchbox world to take home.

RECIPE 21

Cave Rave

Ingredients:
- Potting on tray
- Wall basket liner
- Moss, greengrocer's grass or similar
- Pieces of ivy
- Twigs
- Rocks, pebbles
- Cave inhabitants – the choice is yours!

Method:
Place the moss or greengrocers grass in the base of the tray. Position the basket liner, flat side down, so that you have a cave. Drape the moss, ivy and twigs over the cave to disguise it and make it look more mysterious. Place the rocks and pebbles around the environment.

Why not…
Keep an old diary near this small world so that children can record their adventures in it, through drawing, mark making or writing.

RECIPE 22

Teletubby fun

Ingredients:
- Builder's tray
- Hanging basket liner
- Moss
- Toy Teletubbies
- Toy rabbits
- Some small pots of daisies, when available.

Method:
Spread the moss over the base of the builder's tray. Cut a door in the hanging basket liner and place it on the tray so that it looks like a Teletubby House. Add the pots of daisies, covering the pots with more moss, so that it looks like the daisies are growing in the garden. Add the Teletubbies and the rabbits.

Why not…
Keep some Teletubby comics near the small world, for the children to read and look at. Show an episode from a Teletubby video or DVD. Let the children tell you about their favourite parts. Let them join in with the songs and stories.

Digging around

Ingredients:

- A deep container, such as a gravel tray or an under the bed box.
- Compost or some other suitable digging medium.
- Some diggers and trucks
- Small construction figures
- Some yellow construction helmets
- Small pieces of piping – sawn lengths of drainpipe would be suitable.

Method:

Add the compost to the deep container; making sure that there is sufficient to provide enough 'work' for the diggers. Now add the diggers, trucks, construction figures and the pieces of piping. Leave the construction helmets near the small world so that children can wear them when they play.

Why not…

Substitute the compost for rather unusual medium… dog biscuits! These are very satisfying to use with trucks and diggers, as they make a wonderful noise when being loaded and unloaded.

Recommended Read: Dazzling Diggers, Tony Mitton, Kingfisher Books, ISBN 0753403501

RECIPE 24

Time for a Rhyme

Ingredients:

- Detergent tablet boxes
- Wrapping paper
- Small props linked to a popular rhyme or song that the children know well.

Method:

Cover the box in wrapping paper. You might wish to link this to the rhyme that is inside the box, but this is not always possible (or necessary!) Add the objects, and perhaps a copy of the rhyme, typed up and laminated. For example, a small world set for 'The Wheels on the Bus' might include a piece of road map, folded up for the children to use as a base, at least one toy bus and some passengers.

Why not...

Involve parents in putting together a collection of these boxes. Brainstorm ideas for the contents with them. It will give you a great opportunity to explain the value of both small world play and rhyme and song. Then you could use them as part of a home lending scheme for literacy activities.

RECIPE 25

Every picture tells a story

Ingredients:

- Postcards or posters of famous paintings.
- A selection of objects that relate to that painting. (N.B these could be selected by the children, after discussion with you)
- Construction equipment
- A variety of fabric

Method:
Discuss the painting with the children. Imagine what kind of world might exist beyond and around the painting. Let the children create the world with the resources provided. (They may need more 'ingredients than have been suggested here.)

Why not…
Try this activity with some abstract paintings as well as those that obviously depict a particular kind of landscape or environment.
Add some toy people, so that they can have an adventure in the land of the painting.

Recommended Read: Katie's Picture Show, by James Mayhew, Orchard Books, ISBN 1843623978

RECIPE 26

Get Set!

Ingredients:
- A tray
- A packet of green jelly
- A collection of small dinosaurs
- Some artificial pondweed
- A jelly mould, bowl or similar container.

Method:
Make up the jelly according to the instructions on the packet. Place the dinosaurs and artificial pondweed into the jelly mould or bowl. Pour the jelly mix over and allow it to set. When the jelly is set, dip the mould *very quickly* into a sink of warm water and turn the jelly out on to the tray. The children can then demolish the jelly to reveal the dinosaurs and the plants, which will then be in their very own rather unusual swamp.

N.B If you feel that it is inappropriate to use jelly for this activity, it can also be done with gelatine and water coloured with food colouring.

Why not…
Change the colours of the jelly, and the contents! It might be exciting to have a jelly full of spiders or worms!

Recommended Read: Saturday Night at The Dinosaur Stomp, Carol Diggory Shields, Walker Books, ISBN 0744563453

Flowerpot men – or women!

Ingredients:

- A selection of flowerpots – some clay, some plastic, and a variety of different sizes.
- Compost
- Pebbles
- Play people
- Toy animals
- A square gravel tray.

Method:

Spread the compost throughout the gravel tray so that it is deep enough to wedge the flowerpots in when they are placed on their side. Add the flowerpots in whichever way you like, arranging them so that they resemble a small community of dwellings. Put in the people and the animals. Show the children how to make paths between the houses using the pebbles.

Why not…

Replace the compost with moss, to give the environment a different feel.
Get the children to tape record the stories that they tell.

RECIPE 28

I'm a little teapot!

Ingredients:
- A large, old, teapot, preferably metal! (This prevents possible breakages)
- Some small cuddly animals, either toys or finger puppets (mice would be ideal)
- A handful of shredded paper (optional)

Method:
Pop the shredded paper, if using, into the teapot and add the cuddly mice. Mix together, so that the mice are hidden!

Why not...
Wrap the whole lot up in a brown paper parcel addressed to the children and leave them to discover and unwrap it.

An Octopuses Garden 'neath The Sea

Ingredients:

- A builder's tray
- A large sheet of bubble wrap
- Shells
- Seaweed (real or artificial)
- Several toy octopi, some toy fish
- Glass nuggets
- Attractive, shiny pebbles
- Water

Method:

Completely cover the base of the builder's tray in bubble wrap. This will give the small world an interesting look. Pour in the water on top of this. Add the glass nuggets and the pebbles, the shells and the seaweed. To complete the underwater environment add the octopi and their fishy companions

Why not…

Add some toy sharks to increase tension and add a bit of spice to the adventures.

Recommended Read: The Rainbow Fish, by Marcus Pfister, North South Books, ISBN 1558585362

RECIPE 30

Honey, I shrunk the kids…

Ingredients:

- Potting up tray
- Hanging basket moss or compost or pea shingle, etc
- Large log
- Giant sized toy insects
- Artificial flowers (not absolutely necessary!!)
- A selection of tall grasses
- A small pot of ivy – or two!
- Some toy children

Method:
Spread the substance that you have chosen for the base all over the potting up tray. Add the large log and the grasses along with the artificial flowers, if using. Position the giant sized insects and the small children. Wait for the stories to start!

Why not…
Write a letter to the children in your setting, pretending to be from the characters in the small world, asking for help. Can the children think of a way to help them escape? How can they protect themselves from, say, the giant spider?

Recommended Read: In The Tall, Tall Grass, Denise Fleming, Red Fox, ISBN 0099131714

RECIPE 31

Snail Trail

Ingredients:

- Gravel tray
- Lots of toy snails
- Some cabbage leaves
- Compost
- Stones
- Large pieces of bark
- A flowerpot or two

Method:

Spread the compost out in the gravel tray. Add the large pieces of bark, stones, and flowerpots, lying on their sides. Scatter some cabbage leaves on the surface of the small world. (N.B. These will need renewing regularly if you intend to keep the small world out for any length of time.) Position the snails in various parts of the miniature environment.

Why not…

Use a hand held plant sprayer to spray water on the small world to make it slightly damp.

Alternatively, for a truly slimy experience, mix up some cornflour paste with water and green food colouring. Pour into a tray and add the snails – watch those trails appear, as the children push them through the mixture!

Recommended Read: The Snail House, by Allan Ahlberg, Walker Books, ISBN 0744582318

RECIPE 32

Ant attack

Ingredients:
- 'Under the bed' box, preferably one made of clear plastic, but it really doesn't matter.
- Some greengrocer's grass
- Some potting compost
- Large chunks of wood
- Small twigs
- Leaves and leaf skeletons
- Pebbles and stones
- A whole lot of toy ants

Method:
Add compost to the 'under the bed' box, until it is quite deep. Spread some greengrocer's grass over half the surface, so that the ants can operate under and over ground. Position the large chunks of wood, pebbles and stones throughout. Sprinkle the leaf skeletons across the top. Finally, add the ants!

Why not…
Teach the children to sing 'The ants came marching one by one.'

Recommended Read: Amazing Anthony Ant, by Lorna Philpott, Dolphin, ISBN 1858812844

RECIPE 33

Film pot people

Ingredients:
- Film pot/s
- Fimo or similar modelling material
- Glitter
- Water
- Sequins

Method:
Fashion two people per pot from Fimo. You may wish to make tiny indents in the face for features. It is a good idea to warm it in your hands first. Following the instructions on the Fimo make sure that the people are set.
Carefully pour some water into the film pot and add the little people and a sprinkling of glitter. Then add some sequins. It needn't be very many.
Use this as an example to help the children make their own little film pot people.

Why not…
Talk with the children about the little people that they have created. Encourage them to give them names, and to talk about their characters. Maybe they might like to come out of the film pot and into a small container such as a saucer – to have some little adventures.

RECIPE 34

Book it!

Ingredients:
A thick, old book. It will need to have a hard cover, but will not need to be a book for children.
A sharp craft knife (don't worry – this is not for the children's use)
A collection of characters, from a story that the children know well. (These will need to be fairly small)

Method:
Open up the book and turn over the frontispiece. Draw a rectangle on the first page, leaving a suitable margin around the edge. Using the craft knife cut out the rectangle on as many pages as you need in order to make a hole (secret compartment!!) in the book. This will take some time, as it needs to be done carefully, but the end result is more than worth it!
Pop your selection of characters into the book and close the cover.
Leave it where the children will discover it. Help them re-enact the story with the small toys.

Why not...
Once the children have been introduced to the activity, you can vary it as much as you like! You may wish to change the characters on a weekly basis. Ensure that you allow the children to create new version of the stories that they have heard. Being a stickler for accuracy will not help the children's imaginations grow!

RECIPE 35

Material World

Ingredients:

- Several pieces of fabric, of varying sizes, colours and kinds. You might include velvet, corduroy and net – but any random selection of fabric will do.
- Pieces or ribbon, bias binding and lace
- Buttons, beads and sequins
- Selection of animals and people

Method:

Spread the fabric out in a suitable place, where is room for the children to play comfortably, on the floor or on a tabletop. Leave the other ingredients nearby, so that the children can use them at their will.

Why not…

Watch how the children choose to use the different fabrics and spend time discussing their choices and decisions with them.

Develop this activity through offering children the opportunity to make collages with self-chosen pieces of fabric. They could enhance them with drawings or by attaching interesting artefacts.

Recommended Read: The Patchwork Quilt, Valerie Flournoy, Puffin Books, ISBN 0140554335

Down by the Riverside

Ingredients:

- A long, rectangular gravel tray, or growbag tray.
- Greengrocer's grass, or other green fabric.
- Blue foil, blue fabric, wool, raffia etc.
- River dwelling animals and birds
- A selection of play people
- Boats, etc.

Method:

Line the tray with the greengrocer's grass or other green fabric. Carefully position the materials that are representing the river, so that it appears to be flowing through the fields. Add the animals, birds, play people and boats.

Why not...

Alter the environment so that is becomes an African river, or an Indian river instead. Discuss with the children how the environment could be altered and what would need to be different. It would be lovely to make a river with elephants bathing in it!

Recommended Read; Mr.Gumpy's Outing, by John Burningham, Red Fox ISBN0099408791

RECIPE 37

Mud, mud glorious mud

Ingredients:

- Under the bed box
- A small bag of Sterilised compost
- Artificial pond weeds (if desired)
- Toy hippopotami (plastic)
- Some large smooth pebbles
- Large pieces of bark.
- Water

Method:

Tip as much of the compost as you need into the 'under the bed box'. Add water until you get a lovely muddy consistency. Position the pebbles, weed and bark. Finally, add the hippopotami.

Why not…

Add some crocodiles, for added excitement.

Carefully add water to the small world so that the hippos can swim with their legs under the water just as they do in Africa.

Swap the hippopotami for a large group of pigs, or other animals that enjoy a muddy environment.

Recommended Read: Hot Hippo, by Mwenye Hadithi, Hodder, ISBN 0340413913

RECIPE 38

Magical mystery tour

Ingredients:

- A builder's tray
- Box of soap flakes
- Silver and gold glitter
- Gold and/or silver spray paint
- A variety of bare twigs
- Plasticene
- Toy unicorns

Method:

Firstly, prepare the twigs. Spread some old newspaper on the floor or on a table, place the twigs on the newspaper and spray them gold, silver or a mixture of both. Allow them to dry. When the twigs are dry, wedge them into a large ball of plasticene so that they will stand up in the builder's tray. Now sprinkle the soap flakes all over the builder's tray until the surface is thickly covered with flakes. Add as much glitter as you like, to make it look magical. Next, place the trees in the builder's tray, pressing the plasticene down hard. Add the unicorns and hey presto! You have a very magical environment.

Why not...

Add some tinsel to the trees to add to the magical atmosphere

Place a small wooden treasure chest containing beads or small jewels beneath one of the trees

Recommended Read: Nobody Rides The Unicorn, by Adrian Mitchell, Picture Corgi, ISBN 0552546178

Toadstool Treasures

Ingredients:
- A selection of replica mushrooms and toadstools – these might come in a variety of shapes, sizes and materials. They may be wooden, ceramic or spun paper.
- A potting on tray
- Some greengrocer's grass
- Two or three pots of grasses (optional)
- Some finger puppet fairies and/or some toy insects
- A handful of coloured glass nuggets

Method:
Spread the greengrocer's grass over the base of the potting on tray. Add pots of grasses, if using, by positioning them at the back of the tray. Then add the toadstools, the fairies and the insects. Sprinkle glass nuggets across the green grocers grass to add to the magical atmosphere.

Why not…
Encourage the children to write letters to the fairy creatures.
Will they write back?

Recommended Read: Jethro Byrde, Fairy Child, by Bob Graham, Walker Books ISBN 1844284824

RECIPE 40

A Super Swamp

Ingredients:

- A large cat litter tray (unused of course)
- Moss (the sort sold to line hanging baskets is ideal)
- Toy crocodiles and snakes
- Water
- Ferns in pots

Method:

Spread the moss out in the cat litter tray and add enough water to make it nice and squelchy. Position the ferns in their pots around the tray to add to that swampy atmosphere. Add the animals.

Why not…

Replace the crocodiles and snakes with frogs and toads. Add large pieces of driftwood for added interest.

Recommended Read: Harry and the Dinosaurs Romp in the Swamp, Ian Whybrow, Puffin Books, ISBN 0140569847

RECIPE 41

Walking on the moon

Ingredients:
- A grow bag tray
- Some assorted rigid plastic containers (e.g. bowls, Tupperware boxes etc), say three or four.
- Some white gravel
- An old white sheet
- Astronauts
- Junk modelling materials
- Silver foil

Method:
First make your lunar module from junk modelling material. Make sure that you ask the children to help you. You can use the silver foil to cover the junk models, to make them look like a wonderful space vehicle. Now you are ready to re- create the moon's surface. Position the rigid plastic containers on the grow bag tray. Drape the white sheet over the containers, so that you are now looking at a surface with contours, hills and bumps. Add some white gravel. This makes a lovely crunchy surface for your astronauts to walk/jump/bounce around on. Finally, add the lunar modules and astronauts.

Why not…
Keep some postcards of views of the Earth from space near this small world to encourage open-ended talk and questioning.

Recommended Read: Whatever Next, by Jill Murphy, Picturemac, ISBN 033363621X

RECIPE 42

Logging on

Ingredients:
A large slice of log, rubbed with sandpaper to prevent splinters.
Some natural materials, e.g. moss, leaves, petals, flowers, small twigs, pebbles
Tiny figures or animals of the children's choice

Method:
Place the log where the children can have easy access to it. Arrange the natural materials nearby and explain to the children that they can create a small world on the log – and it can be anything that they want it to be.

Why not…
Have more than one slice of log available so that various groups of children can create small worlds, and they can be used together, so that characters from the different 'log worlds' can interact with one another.

The Dragon's Lair

Ingredients:
- A gravel tray
- Coloured sand – orange or red would be particularly effective.
- Gold glitter
- Toy dragons
- Pebbles
- Rocks
- Alabaster eggs

Method:
Spread the coloured sand all over the gravel tray; make it as deep as is practical. Add the golden glitter. Build a nest or a lair with the rocks and pebbles and position the alabaster eggs nearby – or inside, depending on how you have created the lair/nest. Add the dragons.

Why not…
Add some toy knights to the scene, or a toy princess, or a wizard.
Use blue or green sand to create the lair of a sea dragon. You might also want to add some dried seaweed and some shells.

Recommended Read 'The Dragon of an Ordinary Family' by Margaret Mahy, Mammoth 0749737425

Nest

Ingredients:

- Coir fibre, or raffia
- Twigs or small branches
- Some toy birds
- A few polystyrene eggs
- Some feathers
- Square gravel tray

Method:

Spread the twigs and small branches over the surface of the gravel tray.
Fashion a nest with the coir and or raffia. Add the eggs and finally, the birds!

Why not…

Colour or decorate the eggs with the children. Make some enormous eggs by covering balloons with papier – mache – whose eggs could they be? Make a nest in sand and replace birds with lizards, snakes or other egg-laying creatures.

Recommended Read: The Egg, M.P. Robertson, Frances Lincoln, ISBN 071121525

RECIPE 45

Hats Off

Ingredients:

- An old hat.
- A collection of small toys – a mixture of people and animals would be good
- A selection of objects such as cotton reels, buttons, ribbons, etc
- An old head scarf (optional)

Method:

Place all the objects and the scarf, if using, inside the hat. Leave the rest up to the children!

Why not…

Collect a variety of hats, and let the children choose the small world toys to go in them.

Recommended Read 'The Quangle Wangle's Hat' by Edward Lear, available in poetry anthologies for young children

RECIPE 46

Bottling it up

Ingredients:
- Screw top, clear plastic bottle.
- Water
- Food Colouring
- Cooking oil;
- Novelty sequins (easily obtainable from party suppliers and stationery shops)
- Sand (optional)
- Small shells (optional)

Method:
Pour some water into the bottle, not quite filling it to the top. Add some food colouring, cooking oil and novelty sequins. If using sand and small shells, it is a good idea to put these in the bottle first, before adding the other ingredients. Shake the bottle and watch what happens!

Why not…
Make a small collection of these small worlds, using different colours and different kinds of sequins.
Involve the children in choosing the ingredients for the 'world in a bottle'.

RECIPE 47

Sandcastle Street

Ingredients:

- A grow bag tray
- Sand
- A selection of flowerpots, yoghurt pots, etc.
- Some small toys to live in the street – these can be people, but they don't have to be!
- Some small sticks, pieces of coloured paper, ribbon, feathers, tiny shells, etc.
- Small vehicles (optional)

Method:

Place the sand in the tray. Encourage the children to build a little row of houses down each long side of the tray, using the flowerpots and yoghurt cartons. They can embellish the houses by making little signs, adding feathers, dried flowers and shells if they wish to. Then add some characters to inhabit the street and some adventures can begin immediately.

Why not…

Use this small world for maths by putting numbers on the houses.

Keep some bookmaking equipment nearby so that children can record the adventures that take place in the street.

RECIPE 48

Worming your way in

Ingredients:
- Some potting compost
- A long, shallow gravel tray
- A selection of elastic bands
- Various lengths of electrical wire and/or electrical wire covering. (available from DIY stores)
- Pinecones
- Large flat slabs of stone or rock
- Chunky pieces of wood or bark

Method:
Heap the potting compost into the tray and spread it out. Snip the elastic bands with a pair of scissors, so that they become stretchy lengths of elastic resembling earthworms. Cut the electric wires into a variety of lengths. Add your very exciting worms to the compost. You may wish to hide some completely, half bury some and leave others on the surface. Place the stones and bark in the small world.

Why not…
Listen out for all the mathematical language that the children use when playing with this small world. You may be surprised!
Bury a piece of Fool's Gold in the compost. See what occurs!

Twinkle Twinkle

Ingredients:
- Silver Foil
- Tinsel, in a variety of colours
- As many attractive shiny objects as you can find – create some by spraying old toys and artefacts with silver or gold spray paint.
- Tin cans, washed, and ensuring that any rough edges have been removed.
- Any suitable container, depending on the scale of the toys that have been chosen.

Method:
Cover the base that you are using in silver foil. Add the tinsel, and the shiny objects and toys.

Why not…
Offer the children different kinds of lenses and magnifying glasses to look at the world through.

RECIPE 50

Mirror, Mirror

Ingredients:
A large childproof mirror, or a mirror tile placed on soft fabric inside a square gravel tray.
A small selection of animals and/or people chosen by the children
A collection of artefacts with which to create scenery, e.g. small trees from cake decorating shops etc.

Method:
Place the mirror or mirror tile where the children can have safe, easy access to it. Add the other ingredients!

Why not…
Use novelty mirror tiles such as those available from IKEA, to create a slightly different world.

Recommended Read: Through The Magic Mirror, Anthony Browne, Walker Books ISBN 0744577071

We hope you have found this publication useful.   Other titles in our 'Exciting Things To Do' series are:

For details on these and all our other early years resources visit our website: www.educationalpublications.com